August 1, 1980

To Bon and Susan Caravello,
with the best wishes of
Walter C. Zangram

CINCINNATI
IN COLOR

Profiles of America

CINCINNATI

in Color

Text, and Notes
on the Illustrations by

WALTER CONSUELO LANGSAM

President Emeritus of the University of Cincinnati

A Collection of Color Photographs by

JULIANNE WARREN

HASTINGS HOUSE · PUBLISHERS

New York, 10016

PUBLISHED 1978 BY HASTINGS HOUSE, PUBLISHERS, INC.

Reprinted February, 1979
Reprinted April, 1980

Library of Congress Cataloging in Publication Data
Langsam, Walter, Consuelo, 1906–
 Cincinnati in color.

 (Profiles of America)
 1. Cincinnati—Description. 2. Cincinnati—History.
I. Warren, Julianne. II. Title.
F499.C54L35 1978 977.1'78 78-2543
ISBN 0-8038-1248-5

Published simultaneously in Canada by
Saunders of Toronto, Ltd., Don Mills, Ontario

Printed and bound in Hong Kong by Mandarin Publishers Limited

Dedicated with gratitude for their help to the Director
and Staff of the Cincinnati Historical Society

CONTENTS

The Queen City of the West

THOSE WHO never have been in Cincinnati, who do not know it and only know *of* it, are prone to think of it as merely another midwestern city, with a busy riverfront, a half-million inhabitants, some diversified industry, and a name that is almost impossible to spell correctly. In reality, Cincinnati *is* this and much more. To those who know it and hence hold it in affection, Cincinnati also is a state of mind, reflected in a distinctive outlook and manifested in distinctive behavior. And this distinctiveness, as so often is the case where there is distinctiveness, has elicited diverse and even conflicting characterization by visitors who, in the nearly two centuries since its founding, have been in the city and given oral or written expression to their observations.

General the Marquis de Lafayette, one of whose descendants as late as 1978 made Cincinnati his home during several months of the year, was charmed by the city and its hospitable people during a visit in 1825. Frances Trollope, *the* English Mrs. Trollope of later literary fame, on the other hand, thoroughly disliked the "rough and uncouth" residents, with their "strange practices" and their failure properly to appreciate and patronize the bizarre Bazaar that she built and operated from 1828 to 1830. The whole venture, she wrote, was a waste of the family's "time, health, and money." Amusingly, one of the regional traits that aroused her ire was the unwillingness of the citizenry to buy at the Bazaar the wares that she purchased locally at retail cost and then offered for sale at a goodly mark-up in price.

9

Twelve years after Mrs. Trollope's departure, her countryman, Charles Dickens, called Cincinnati "a beautiful city" and characterized its then nearly "fifty thousand souls" as being "intelligent, courteous, and agreeable," and imbued with a just pride in their municipality. Henry Wadsworth Longfellow labelled Cincinnati the "Queen of the West," and Winston Spencer Churchill, visiting in 1932, referred to it as the most beautiful inland city in the United States.

During the 1960s and 1970s, *Fortune* and *Life* magazines, respectively, praised Cincinnati's effective city-manager government and police force; *Time* called it "dowdy;" and *The Christian Science Monitor* ranked it high among the country's "most livable" cities. A series of national public-opinion polls, taken in the 1970s among businessmen and ambitious younger executives, usually showed Cincinnati among the first ten of desirable cities in which to live and work; the negative views were expressed mainly by persons who never had been there.

But the true Cincinnatians themselves, not especially concerned with others' opinions, cherish their city, even when, from time to time, they "gripe" about it. Indeed, the suburban dwellers who work in Cincinnati proper and enjoy its cultural and recreational offerings, when asked by outsiders where they live, unlike their counterparts in the New York, Chicago, and other metropolitan areas almost invariably say Cincinnati, instead of giving the names of their specific and sometimes exclusive suburban homesites. And the family names of many of the early settlers still may be found among the current listings in the telephone directories.

Cincinnati, with justification, variously has been labelled the northernmost southern city and the southernmost northern city. There is evident in the daily intercourse among its residents and in their reception of visitors much of the graciousness, charm, and courtesy traditionally associated with the South; at the same time, the pace of life and activity resembles that of bustling northern cities. The Queen City, moreover, while offering most of the opportunities found in a metropolis, has retained many of the amenities of small-town living. The people tend to be conservative in business, politics, and moral outlook; but they are quite ready to seek the benefits of sensible and profitable change and progress. Business and professional success is held in high esteem, but religion, education, cultural offerings, and spectator sports rank only slightly lower among local priorities.

Industry and the private citizenry are national pace-setters in contributions to United Appeal campaigns and other worthwhile charities. The Fine Arts Fund (which provides subsidies to the Cincinnati Symphony Orchestra, the Summer Opera, the Cincinnati Museum of Art, the Taft Museum, the Cincinnati Ballet Company, the Playhouse-in-the-Park, the May Festival of choral music, and the Contemporary Arts Center) is generously supported by corporate and private donors. The University of Cincinnati, founded in 1819, Xavier University, founded in 1831, and several smaller local colleges long have enjoyed the community's financial backing in their rise to educational distinction. There is, in short, proven willingness to be one's brother's keeper, without necessarily becoming his general manager.

One special aspect of Cincinnati's development, shared in some degree by other midwestern cities, is the result of a sizable German influx in the nineteenth century. The city in the earlier 1800s attracted large numbers of settlers from the eastern, middle-Atlantic, and southern states, and then from Ireland; but in the 1830s, 1840s, and 1850s many Germans, especially from Bavaria, Württemberg, and the Rhineland, discontented because of political and economic difficulties in their homeland, were lured to Cincinnati as the largest community west of the Allegheny Mountains, as a prosperous inland port, and as the very center in the American West of manufacturing, commerce, meat-packing, beer-brewing, and viticulture. By the time of the outbreak of war in 1861, these German-born immigrants comprised nearly 30 percent of "Zinzinnati's" population.

A section of the city, situated north of the Miami Canal that later was roofed over to become Central Parkway, came to be and still is called Over-the-Rhine. There, many proprietary store shields even today carry unmistakably German family names, and the churches resemble the high, narrow religious structures found in many German villages. This, incidentally, is not at all astonishing when it is noted that the 1890 City Directory listed 89 saloonkeepers alone "whose names begin with 'Sch,' including Schaefer, Schemp, Schneider, Schneidhorst, Schnittker, Schroth, Schwab, and Schweinberger."

From the mid-nineteenth century until World War I, all public schools taught German, and there remain some third- and fourth-generation natives who speak English with an old-country mixture of v's and w's, and who, when they have missed something in conversation, say "Please?" instead of the more customary "Beg your pardon?" Bratwürste and Mettwürste (or "Brats" and "Metts"), Sauerkraut, Schnitzel, and Sauerbraten continue to be staples whenever *gemütliche* Cincinnatians go picnicking, and the annual German *Bierfest* on Fountain Square serves as a memorable nostalgic and gustatory tribute to the citizenry's German origins. It also is to this heritage, and to the contributions of the numerically small but civic-minded and active Jewish element in the population, that must go much of the credit for Cincinnati's educational and cultural appreciation and eminence.

And now, let us turn to some specifics of the city's two centuries of history.

At the close of the Revolutionary War, Great Britain ceded to the new nation a vast and rich land lying between the Appalachian Mountains and the Mississippi River. The "Ohio Country" was part of this Northwest Territory, which included roughly the area covered by the present states of Ohio, Indiana, Illinois, Michigan, and Wisconsin. A framework of government was established for the whole territory by an act of the Continental Congress called the Northwest Ordinance of 1787, itself in many ways a revolutionary document. It prohibited slavery north of the Ohio River; proclaimed freedom of religion; provided for the support of public education through mandatory land grants; and established as a matter of law a new concept in colonialism, namely, that when certain conditions, such as population size, were met, segments of the territory could form states eligible for admission to the Union on an equal footing with the thirteen original states.

But even before the adoption of the Northwest Ordinance, individuals and families had begun to explore the territory, with a view to settlement. Thus, early in 1786, Benjamin Stites, a former officer in the Revolution and a trader from New Jersey, explored the Ohio Country. As he moved southward between the Great and the Little Miami Rivers, he was struck by the beauty and fertility of the land.

Stites was unable to develop this land himself, but his enthusiasm inspired John Cleves Symmes, a fellow-Jerseyite and a member of the Continental Congress, to consider it for investment purposes. Symmes made a trip to the Miami Valley in 1787, which convinced him that the area could be developed profitably. He formed the Miami Land Company, and purchased from the National Government all the land lying between the two Miami rivers northward from the Ohio River to the present site of Lebanon.

Three settlements grew up in the "Symmes Purchase." Columbia, near the present Lunken Airport, was founded on November 18, 1788, when Stites and twenty-six men, women, and children arrived from New Jersey and Pennsylvania. On December 28, 1788, Robert Patterson, John Filson, and Surveyor Israel Ludlow landed with a second group at a cove later known as

Yeatman's Cove, because Griffin Yeatman there opened a tavern; the inlet now is covered by the Riverfront Stadium at the foot of Sycamore Street. Because the party landed across from the mouth of the Licking River in Kentucky, Filson, who had scholarly and poetic inclinations, named the settlement Losantiville, meaning "town opposite the mouth" of the L(icking). In January 1789, Symmes himself established a third, more westerly settlement at North Bend.

It is amusing now to reflect on the limited expansion that some of the early settlers foresaw for their community. Israel Ludlow, for example, recorded in his journal that he "platted the town," marking off the four corners to encompass approximately one square mile. He ran the northern boundary a little less than a mile up from the Ohio River, to today's Seventh Street. And, he wrote, "It (the village) can never grow so as to occupy all the plat, (yet) it is better . . . to aim high. But if the village in the next three or four centuries ever gets up to (Seventh Street), it will be one of the marvels of the world."

Despite physical hardship, disease, crop failures, and Indian attacks, the three settlements survived and grew. In 1789, Major John Doughty selected a high-lying part of Losantiville as the site for a military fort to protect the settlers from the Indians. Construction of the fort was begun immediately, at the eastern edge of what now is downtown Cincinnati, and on December 29, 1789, General John Harmar and two companies of soldiers arrived to garrison the post. Harmar named it Fort Washington, in honor of the nation's first President. At that time, Losantiville consisted of twenty log houses, inhabited by eleven families and twenty-four unmarried men; building lots cost from two dollars to four dollars each.

Arthur St. Clair, Governor of the Northwest Territory, came to inspect Fort Washington soon after its garrisoning. He disliked the name "Losantiville," and, on January 4, 1790, changed it to Cincinnati, in honor of the organization of retired Revolutionary War officers known as the Society of the Cincinnati. On the same day, St. Clair also created Hamilton County, the second to be formed in the Northwest Territory. On St. Patrick's Day, 1790, the first white child was born in Cincinnati. His name was William Moody.

Following several years of bitter warfare throughout the Ohio Country, General "Mad Anthony" Wayne decisively defeated the Indians in the Battle of Fallen Timbers (near Toledo) on August 15, 1794. Under the terms of the Treaty of Greeneville (July 1795), the Wyandot, Delaware, Ottawa, Chippewa, Miami, Wabash, Pottawotamie, Wea, and Piankeshaw Indians surrendered to the

Whites the region comprising approximately the southern two-thirds of present Ohio. With the removal of the Indian danger, the Ohio settlements began to enjoy years of steady growth.

By 1795, Cincinnati had 94 cabins, 10 frame houses, and about 500 inhabitants; the price of building lots had risen to as much as $250. By 1800, the population was up to 750; and in 1805, it numbered 960. Meanwhile, on January 1, 1802, Cincinnati had been incorporated as a town; by this date, also, several appurtenances of town life had been acquired. The Presbyterians built the first church in Cincinnati, and a school was opened in 1792. The first jail, a log cabin, was built in 1793. A number of stores, and even more taverns—there were 70 by 1819—served the townsfolk and the travelers from up and down the river. November 9, 1793, was marked by the appearance of the first newspaper, the *Centinel* (sic) *of the North-Western Territory*, edited, printed, and published by William Maxwell.

Toward the close of the eighteenth century and in the early years of the nineteenth, came a number of settlers who in their own right, and through their descendants, had a lasting impact on Cincinnati. Among these—whose names still are household words in the city—were William Lytle, a friend of Daniel Boone, who came by way of Kentucky; Jacob Burnet from New Jersey; Martin Baum and Mayor David Ziegler, both of German origin; and Nicholas Longworth, Cincinnati's first millionaire.

Martin Baum, a talented businessman and dedicated promoter of civic enterprises—who had a hand in the establishment of the city's first sugar refinery, first iron foundry, first steam flour-mill, first bank, and first central market, and who stimulated the founding of a public library and several musical and literary groups—launched an immigration program that vitally affected the future make-up of Cincinnati's citizenry. Deciding that the community needed the skills and talents of industrious, intelligent, and relatively well-educated immigrants from Germany, he directed his representatives in Philadelphia and Baltimore to seek out desirable Germans who landed there and persuade them to settle in Cincinnati. His initiative thus began a process that made Cincinnati a strongly German community, which, notwithstanding the effects of the so-called melting pot, it remains to this day. By 1810, then, with a population of more than 2,000, Cincinnati was beginning to enjoy an active social life, marked by broad participation in singing societies, amateur theatricals, instrumental-music groups, and the like.

On October 27, 1811, the first steamboat on the western waters, spewing smoke and sparks, arrived at the Public Landing from Pittsburgh. The boat, opener of a new and momentous chapter in the city's history, was the *Orleans*, built for Nicholas J. Roosevelt by Robert Fulton. It demonstrated the potentialities of river navigation by steam when, after going downstream to Louisville at the "incredible" speed of eight miles per hour, it also was able to return to Cincinnati—against the current!

Within a short span of eight years, the lone *Orleans* had grown to a fleet of 70 steamboats plying the rivers between Pittsburgh and New Orleans. Many of these boats were built in Cincinnati, which became, and for three generations or more remained, a major shipbuilding center. In 1840, for example, 33 new riverboats were built in Cincinnati boatyards. Year by year the traffic on the river grew, as the lands to the north, south, and west of Cincinnati filled with settlers.

In one four-month period in 1829, from March to July, some 500 boats tied up at the Public Landing, discharging and taking on passengers; bringing raw materials *from* the East, and carrying *to* the East, the South, and the West the products of Cincinnati's booming industries: tools, furniture, ironware, silverware and pewter, clocks, paper, hats, ready-made clothing, books, flour, beer, whisky, soap, candles, tinware, and pork products. These last, indeed, in the form of bacon, lard, hams, and salt pork, for a time topped the list of shipments. Widely known during this period as "Porkopolis," Cincinnati was at the focal point of the rich corn-growing areas of Ohio, Indiana, and Kentucky, and corn converted to pork (and whisky) was easier, cheaper, and more profitable to haul to distant markets than was corn itself.

This may be as good a place as any for two further observations on the importance of beer in Cincinnati's economy and stomachs. In 1860, the city had 36 beer breweries; together, they shipped some 550,000 gallons of the foamy liquid downriver to Memphis, Vicksburg, Natchez, New Orleans, and points between. In 1893, when beer was exported as far away as the West Indies, Brazil, and Peru—enough remained to provide an average of 40 gallons per person. The 1893 per capita consumption in the Queen City was $2\frac{1}{2}$ times the national average.

The importance of the Ohio River as a channel of commerce, and of Cincinnati as the principal *entrepôt* of the Ohio River Basin, was immeasurably enhanced by the opening of Ohio's canal system, linking the Great Lakes to the river and thence to the South and West. However, within a decade of the completion of the canal system, the harbinger of a change that was to revolutionize transportation and much else besides, and was in time to lessen Cincinnati's orientation toward, and dependence upon, the Ohio River, came into being with the opening in 1841 of the Little Miami Railroad. Its first president was John Jacob Strader, a prominent local steamboat proprietor!

Despite an epidemic of bank failures, a financial depression in 1819, and the Panic of 1837, despite floods and epidemics, the city's phenomenal growth continued with an ever-increasing momentum. The 1819 City Directory—the first to be issued—listed a population of 9,120; in the next eleven years, the city nearly tripled in population, reaching 25,000 in 1830; and nearly doubled again, to 46,000, by 1840. Significantly, 28 percent, or nearly 14,000, of the city's inhabitants in 1840 were born in Germany. In the next twenty years, the population more than tripled, totaling 161,000 in 1860, of whom 44,000, or 27 percent, were of German, and 19,000, or 12 percent, of Irish birth. Physically, too, the city grew. To provide the expanding housing, mercantile, and civic needs, an annual average of more than 300 buildings, mostly of brick, was erected in the 1830s. In 1844, the number of newly-built structures was 1,228.

Clearly having outgrown its town governmental structure by 1819, Cincinnati in that year was incorporated as a city by an act of the state legislature. The new municipal government, although dominated and on occasion even plagued by politics, nevertheless was progressive in its concern for the needs of urban life. From 1839 on, Cincinnati had a municipally-owned water works; and in 1853, the eighteen volunteer fire companies, which exercised a considerable degree of political power in the city, were replaced by a paid municipal fire department, the first of its kind in the United States. It was equipped with newly developed steam fire-engines, many of which were built in Cincinnati.

Daily newspapers, which reflected and created public opinion in the city, had multiplied over the years. By 1841, six English-language and six German-language dailies were being published, supplemented by several religious weeklies, some in English and some in German. Cultural life and public health were enhanced by the founding in 1819 of Cincinnati College, which eventually (1870) grew into the municipal and then (1977) state-owned University of Cincinnati, and by the establishment of numerous medical institutions, each teaching the doctrines of one of the "schools" into which the medical profession then was divided.

Responsible to a high degree for Cincinnati's early emphasis on medicine and public health was Dr. Daniel Drake (1785-1852). Born in New Jersey, Drake first came to Cincinnati in 1800; with a few interruptions to work in Kentucky and study medicine in Philadelphia, he was for nearly half a century a leading physician, scientist, college administrator—and controversial figure in his adopted city. A recent bibliography of his publications in the form of books, articles, speeches, and letters listed some 750 items!

As early as 1810, Drake warned of the danger to health of air pollution from the brickyards, tanneries, and butcheries of the city, a peril that was mitigated only by the many trees that "intercepted" the deleterious fumes. In 1816, he for a time operated a combined drug- and dry-goods store, which contained the first, and very popular, soda fountain west of the Allegheny Mountains. (Cincinnati was responsible for so many "firsts" to the west of these mountains that loyal residents often thank Heaven for the Alleghenies.)

In 1819, Drake persuaded the state legislature to charter Cincinnati College, as well as the Medical College of Ohio in Cincinnati, of which latter he became the first president. Two years later, he induced the state also to establish the Cincinnati Commercial Hospital and Lunatic Asylum, forerunner of the later renowned Cincinnati General Hospital and Cincinnati Medical Center. During the mid-1830s, this "Physician to the West" was chairman of the local chapter of the "Friends of Texas," dedicated to helping the Texans win independence from Mexico.

Lane Seminary, for the training of Presbyterian ministers, was founded in 1829. Lyman Beecher, whose daughter, Harriet Beecher Stowe, in 1852 published *Uncle Tom's Cabin*, became its first president. The Seminary was disrupted by the issue of abolitionism and, in 1834, after a series of heated debates on the subject, half of the student body seceded and migrated northward to strongly abolitionistic Oberlin College. Abolitionism remained a bitterly divisive issue in a community that included in its population large numbers of migrants from the slave states as well as from New England, the largely libertarian German element, and the Irish, who were opposed to abolition from a complex of political, economic, and racial motives. The controversy led to the smashing of presses printing abolitionist literature, and to race riots.

There probably were no Blacks in Hamilton County in 1800. Not long thereafter, however, numbers of free Blacks arrived in Cincinnati as hands on river craft and steamboats; some of them remained in the city, to work as stevedores and in other occupations. By 1826, the black population numbered some 700; in 1829, the figure was about 2,000.

This growth led to increasing difficulty as more and more Irish and German settlers arrived and competed against the Blacks for the available jobs. The year 1829 witnessed a serious race riot, as a consequence of which Ohio's "Black Laws," aimed at restricting Blacks in a variety of ways, were enforced strictly. By 1834, the black population had fallen below one thousand.

Then, as the number of slaves seeking to escape across the Ohio River became sizable, there developed among many Cincinnatians a determination to help them move from "station" to "station" on a so-called Underground Railway, en route to Canada and freedom. Lyman Beecher was active in the movement, and one of his friends, the Quaker, Levi Coffin, came to be recognized as "President of the Underground Railway." Most of the houses that served as stations were fitted with false walls, hidden chambers, tunnels, and the like.

Coffin set up a "Dispatcher's Office" on the northwestern corner of Sixth and Elm Streets, and is credited with having helped some 3,000 slaves in their flight. Among others, he recruited as an aide George Davis, owner of a busy pork-packing plant on lower Sycamore Street. Davis courageously used his business place as a station. The real Eliza, model for Harriet Beecher Stowe's Eliza, was said by some to have found protection after crossing the icy Ohio River at Ripley at a station in the exclusive suburb of Glendale. One group of abolitionists founded an Antislavery Church on West Sixth Street, and this, too, was helpful to runaways.

Meanwhile, William Allen had begun, in 1809, to serve as Cincinnati's first black minister. Fifteen years later, a group of Blacks organized itself as the African Methodist Episcopal Church and worshipped in the Allen Temple, which still stands on the southeastern corner of Broadway and Sixth Street.

Other forms of help to Blacks came from a number of sources. Theodore Weld and some of his fellow-students at Lane Seminary in 1834 began to operate a school for Blacks two nights a week. Nicholas Longworth established an asylum for black orphans in 1844. The *Cincinnati Gazette* in editorials during 1840 bravely defended the Blacks against many of the unwarranted charges that were leveled against them. Shortly before the Civil War, the Gilmore High School for Blacks was founded. And soon after the close of the war, some concerned individuals built Calvary Methodist Episcopal Church on West Seventh Street with a tunnel network, to be used in the event of a return to slavery. A law of 1887 opened all Cincinnati public schools to black children. Thereafter, the schools specifically for Blacks, operated since pre-Civil War days by a special board of education headed by a White, gradually passed out of existence.

Jacob G. Schmidlapp, who had made a fortune in whisky, once said that he "was appalled by the condition in which the (Blacks) were housed." Accordingly, he began in 1911 to build groups of low-cost apartment units in Walnut Hills and in the political enclave of Norwood. Rents were based on ability to pay and normally were set at one day's pay for one week's rent. (The average charged by other landlords was the equivalent of 25-35 percent of the tenants' income.)

The building project was continued to 1924, some years after Schmidlapp's death. The occupancy rate was remarkably high and defaults in rental payments were rare. This "Cincinnati Plan" of inexpensive housing for the poor became the model for similar projects in a number of larger cities. Schmidlapp also established co-operative groceries among the units, erected the Gordon Hotel for Blacks in 1916—it was remodeled into apartments some twenty years later, and established scholarship funds to help poor children of all races gain a good education.

The pre-Civil War years were more than an era of spectacular material development; during them were planted also the seeds of Cincinnati's future political, social, artistic, and cultural development. As the leading metropolis of the Midwest, Cincinnati reflected and frequently affected all the political issues of the growing United States. The first of its citizens to become President of the United States, William Henry Harrison, "Old Tippecanoe," was elected to that post in 1840. (His grandson, President Benjamin Harrison, was born in a suburb of Cincinnati, but made his career in Indianapolis.) In future years, in 1876 and 1912, respectively, two other Cincinnatians, Rutherford B. Hayes and William Howard Taft, were to be similarly honored; and several other Cincinnatians, among them Salmon P. Chase and Robert A. Taft, were widely regarded as "presidential timber."

Cincinnati early became a major midwestern publishing center. Despite limitations of space, reference here must be made to one local publishing venture that greatly influenced American education and hundreds of millions of Americans, particularly in rural areas, over a period of nearly five-score years.

The publishing firm of Truman and Smith Company, established in 1834 and destined, after a series of ownership changes, to become the American Book Company in 1890, signed a contract in 1836 with William Holmes McGuffey (who in that year resigned a professorship at Miami University, Ohio, to become

President and Professor of Moral Philosophy at the Cincinnati College) to prepare a primer, four graded readers, and a speller. The resulting little books, eventually to become famous as *McGuffey's Readers*, were attractively bound, illustrated with engaging pictures, joyful in content, and marked by moral instruction. Seven million copies were sold between 1836 and 1850; some 122,000,000 were sold by 1920; and, through several later additions, a total sale of more than 125,000,000 copies was recorded. On the logical assumption that individual copies probably were used by several children, the historian Carl Vitz in 1957 told the McGuffey Federated Societies of America that, "except the Bible, no other book or set of books has influenced the American mind so much."

In the creative arts, too, ante-bellum Cincinnati began to produce or serve as home for leading lights. Hiram Powers, whose artistic education was financed by Nicholas Longworth, achieved fame as a sculptor. His *Greek Slave*, completed in 1843, probably was the most popular statue of the period in both Europe and the United States. Thomas Buchanan Read was known not alone for his painting but for his poetry, in particular for "Sheridan's Ride." In later generations came the widely acclaimed paintings of Frank Duveneck, Henry Farny, Louis Meakin, Elizabeth Nourse, Edward Potthast, Joseph Sharp, John H. Twachtman, and Herman Wessel; the sculptures of Clement J. Barnhorn and Bruce Haswell; the etchings of E.T. Hurley; and the engravings of Caroline Williams.

The rise of such civic-minded captains of industry and finance as Miles Greenwood, Nicholas Longworth, and Jason Evans stimulated a cultural life based on the existence of a cultivated leisured, or at least partially leisured, class. The Literary Club of Cincinnati, still hale and hearty, was founded in 1849. In the same year, the Historical and Philosophical Society of Ohio moved from Columbus to Cincinnati, changing its name to The Cincinnati Historical Society; it, too, has prospered, and remains active as it approaches its sesquicentennial year.

Mention has been made of General Lafayette's memorable visit to Cincinnati in 1825 and Charles Dickens' sojourn there in 1842. William Makepeace Thackeray gave a series of lectures during the early 1850s, as later did Ralph Waldo Emerson. Perhaps outshining all these in glamour was the three-day visit in 1860 of the Prince of Wales, the later King Edward VII; it was said that the tickets to the reception in his honor, priced at $10, were bid up to $200 before the subscriptions were closed. In 1854, Henry Wadsworth Longfellow acknowledged a gift of Catawba wine from Nicholas Longworth, the product of his own vineyards located on southward-facing slopes overlooking the Ohio River, with a poem entitled "Catawba Wine." Its closing lines spoke of the "Queen of the West,/In her garlands dressed,/On the banks of the Beautiful River." And "The Queen City" Cincinnati has remained ever since.

The long period of the city's uninterrupted growth was broken, though only briefly, by the advent of the Civil War. As a largely conservative border community, with close social and economic ties to the South, Cincinnati at first seemed to favor a peaceful separation of the two sections through secession. But the firing on Fort Sumter created an outburst of pro-Union fervor that transcended economic interests and even the pull of the geographic loyalties of many Cincinnatians who (or whose parents) had come to the city from Virginia, the Carolinas, and other seceded states. The male population almost literally "sprang to arms." Open slots in existing militia companies were filled and new regiments were formed. The 5th, 6th, 9th, and 10th Regiments of Ohio Volunteer Infantry were all-Cincinnati units. The 9th Infantry was conspicuous as an all-German "Turner" regiment; indeed, its regimental history, published after the war, was written in German. The Literary Club, which numbered George B. McClellan (who was to became General-in-Chief of the Union armies), John Pope (commander in 1862 of the Army of the Potomac), and Rutherford B. Hayes among its 51 members, voted unanimously to transform itself into a militia drill company. All 51 members entered the Union army and all but one were commissioned; 18 achieved the ranks of lieutenant-colonel, colonel, or general officer; none was killed in battle. After a temporary dislocation, commerce and industry revived and went on to new strength as Cincinnati became the major supply point for the manifold needs of the Union armies operating west of the Alleghenies. Many of the gunboats used by the Union Navy on the Mississippi and the Ohio Rivers and their tributaries to the south were built in Cincinnati. Professor George C. Blackman of the Medical College, who was appointed Union Brigadier Surgeon of Volunteers, produced the first American textbook in military surgery.

Twice during the war, Cincinnati faced the spectre of attack, first in the summer of 1862, with the Braxton Bragg-Kirby Smith invasion of Kentucky, and a year later with John Hunt Morgan's Indiana-Ohio Raid. To protect the city from what was expected to be an invasion by Bragg's and Smith's armies, Major General Lewis Wallace (who, as Lew Wallace, published *Ben Hur* in 1880) and Governor David Tod issued a call to able-bodied male civilians in the city and neighboring counties to construct and man a series of fortifications on the crests of hills on the Kentucky side of the Ohio River. As it happened, the somewhat boisterous effort of these 15,000 rough "Squirrel Hunters" was unneeded, for the invasion failed to materialize. In July 1863, Morgan and 2,000 men, after crossing the Ohio below Louisville, rode along the river through Indiana and entered Ohio at Harrison, in the northwestern corner of Hamilton County. During the night of July 13, he skirted Cincinnati proper and passed through its northern suburbs on his way east to eventual defeat and capture two weeks later.

With the end of the Civil War, the country and Cincinnati with it, entered a new era of expansion. In Cincinnati, a long-planned bridge over the Ohio River to Kentucky became a reality. The agitation to build the bridge had begun in 1845. During the following year, John Augustus Roebling submitted plans for a single-span suspension bridge, using wire cables and stiffened trusses. The project was delayed by controversy, the Panic of 1857, and local financial problems. After the foundations for the towers on both banks were constructed in 1857, no further work was done for six years. When work was resumed in 1863, under Roebling's supervision, it went quickly, and the bridge was opened to traffic on January 1, 1867.

Another event of great, some whimsically would say, even greater, importance from the point of view of its enduring impact on Cincinnati as a community, was the assembling in 1869 of the Cincinnati Red Stocking Base Ball Team, the first all-professional (paid) baseball club. Now known as the Cincinnati Reds, the team has had its "ups and downs," but throughout its good fortunes and bad, it has retained the affection and prideful identification of its constituents. In 1919, 1939, 1940, 1961, 1970, 1972, 1975, and 1976—when the "beloved" Reds won the National League Pennant, and even more in 1919, 1940, 1975, and 1976, when they also won the World Series, they caused most Cincinnatians "to feel several inches taller."

In many ways, the 1870s were a Golden Age in Cincinnati. The population continued to grow, albeit at a declining rate, so that the citizenry could survey the situation and concentrate on the never-ending task of adapting the physical and institutional environments to the needs of urban life. Led by the well-to-do, residents began to move from the basin area to the surrounding hilltop; streetcar lines and steep inclines were built; gas lighting of the streets was standardized; and parks were provided. The railroad system serving the city continued to expand, and although there was a resurgence of riverboat traffic after the end of the Civil War, railroads were becoming the primary mode of transportation for passengers and freight alike.

To retain its position as the primary traffic link between the North and the South, Cincinnati took the unprecedented step, unique to this day, of financing the building of its own railroad, the Cincinnati, New Orleans & Texas Pacific Railway Company, popularly called the Cincinnati Southern Railway. This provided direct connection from Cincinnati and the network of rail lines running to it from the Northwest, North, and Northeast to Chattanooga and beyond; the first Cincinnati-Chattanooga run was made early in 1880. Eventually leased to the Southern Railway System, the line remains prosperous notwithstanding the problems that have beset railroads since the end of World War II. The annual rental payments contribute significantly to the city's revenues. Further to enhance the city's position as an industrial and trading center, the Cincinnati Stock Yards were built and Industrial Expositions became an annual affair beginning in 1870.

Several of the city's present major cultural institutions trace their beginnings to that same fruitful decade. As part of the German immigration in the years following 1830, there came to Cincinnati numbers of German Jews; it was owing to their interest and enterprise that the city eventually became the center of the Reform Judaism movement, led by Rabbi Isaac M. Wise, and the site of Hebrew-Union College, founded in 1875. The Cincinnati Public Library, which in 1898 became the Public Library of Cincinnati and Hamilton County, originally was housed in a small stone opera house dating from 1865. This building was replaced in 1955 by a large, well-designed structure, and the library grew to become one of the best such facilities in the Midwest. The Cincinnati Society of Natural History was organized in 1870. Through the generosity of the Geier Family, associated with the world's largest manufacturer of machine tools, a Museum of Natural History in Eden Park was dedicated in 1958.

The Cincinnati Zoological Garden, or "Zoo," was opened in 1875. It owed its existence to the efforts of the Cincinnati Zoological Society and, in particular, to the generous contributions in money and energy of Andrew Erkenbrecher. This prosperous starch manufacturer retired from business so as to have sufficient time to make an "animal park" a reality. Interestingly, Sol Stephan, the animal trainer who delivered the elephant, Conqueror, to the Zoo, and who planned to stay for only "a few days," remained actively connected with that institution for sixty-two years, retiring at last in 1937. So has Cincinnati, over many scores of years, similarly appealed to other, though not always so long-lived, persons who planned to reside in the Queen City temporarily for business or educational reasons, and then made it their permanent home.

The famous Conservatory of Music and College of Music were founded, respectively, in 1867 and 1878. They merged to become the College-Conservatory of Music in 1955 and, after a major fund-raising campaign, became a school of the University of Cincinnati seven years later. This university, absorber of Cincinnati College and several other institutions, itself was chartered under state law in 1870 as a municipal institution, and in 1977 became a state university. It is discussed further on the page facing a picture of its McMicken Hall.

The Cincinnati Observatory, whose German-made twelve-inch refractor telescope then was the largest in the United States, and which was dedicated in 1843 by ex-President John Quincy Adams on a hilly site (on Mount Ida, later named Mount Adams) donated by Nicholas Longworth, I, was moved in 1873-1875 to Observatory Place. The new site at Mount Lookout, donated by John Kilgour, was relatively free from the disturbing smoke and other industrial obstacles to astronomical observations that beleaguered Mount Adams. Operation of the Cincinnati Observatory was entrusted by the city to the University of Cincinnati.

From its earliest days, Cincinnati's German community has been addicted to music in all its forms. German musical societies of all sorts, choral and instrumental, were organized from the earliest days of the arrival of Germans in the city. The first *Männerchor* was formed in 1838, and within a few years it and other German choral groups were hosts to *Sängerfesten* in which similar German choral groups from Louisville, Indianapolis, Columbus, and other cities participated. In 1873, the first "Cincinnati Music Festival" was held, with an orchestra of 108 musicians and a chorus of 700, made up of members of the 36 choral societies throughout the United States that had accepted invitations to take part. The festival was so successful that it was decided to make it a biennial event. It has retained its vitality; renamed the May Festival and eventually held annually, it remains one of the major elements of the ever-crowded musical life of the community. Its move, in 1878, to a permanent home is described in the text facing the picture of the Music Hall.

In the late nineteenth and early twentieth centuries, Cincinnati was a bustling industrial city with a wide variety of locally-owned business enterprises,

24

which contributed then and later to an usually stable economy. Many of these industries were founded before or during the Civil War by newcomers to the city from the East and from Europe, and they were developed into major companies by the second, third, and fourth generations of the same families.

The entrepreneurs included the Procters and the Gambles, first in candles, then in soap, and later still in detergents and diversified home products; the Brunswicks and the Balkes in billiard tables; the Gruens in watches; the Wurlitzers and Baldwins in musical instruments; the Heekins in tin cans. Also, the Fleischmanns in yeast and gin; the Erkenbrechers in starch; the Powells and the Lunkenheimers (later Lunkens) in valves and in brass and bronze castings; the Werks and the Jergens in soap and in toilet soap and cosmetics, respectively; the Emerys in candles, animal fats, and later chemicals; the Geiers, LeBlonds, and Christensens in machine tools; the Aults in printing inks; and the Seasongoods and Friedlanders in men's ready-to-wear clothing.

And there were many more: brewers, furniture manufacturers, silversmiths, boat builders, printers and publishers, pork packers, and makers of fire engines, carriages and automobile bodies, shoes, playing cards, paper, and so on and on. All these were able to recruit from a large and growing pool of stable skilled workers. As has been indicated, here were produced also the scores of millions of McGuffey's *Readers*; and it was from these and Cincinnati teacher William Ray's arithmetic and algebra texts that several generations of Americans learned the three R's. Thus, in good times and bad, Cincinnati produced some of nearly everything needed by the rapidly-growing nation and its expanding economy. This broad band of manufacturers, and Cincinnati's favorable geographic location helped make Cincinnati by 1873 the third largest railroad switching center in the country, with a local railway labor force of 6,000. The number of "hands" employed in the Queen City in 1880 was 75,000; in 1970, the figure was 140,000.

With prosperity, however, came all the problems that plague large and growing cities. Municipal services—sanitation, street cleaning, water supply and sewers, transportation—all lagged behind the expanding needs. At the same time, there flourished the usual negative concomitants of urban life—slums, crime, prostitution, poverty, and disease. Cincinnati in the post-Civil War decades was known throughout the South as a "wide-open town." During one nine-day stretch in 1883, nine local murders were committed. The going rate at the time for corpses sold to the Medical College was $15.00 per body.

Much of this negative aspect was related to that common bane of American cities, large and small, in the era from approximately 1870-1920, namely, a corrupt, boss-ridden municipal government. The Queen City's "Boss" was George B. Cox, who, from 1884 until his death in 1916, in effect *was* the government of Cincinnati. Through such lieutenants as the jovial August Herrmann and the smooth-mannered but tough Rudolph (Rud) Hynicka, and with a corrupt judiciary, rigged elections, graft, and toleration by an acquiescent or intimidated business community, Cox, a one-time owner of the Reds baseball club, not alone ran Cincinnati, but became a power in state and national politics.

Not until after World War I, several years after Cox's death, did a small group of business and professional men organize a reform group called the Cincinnatus Association, which, incidentally, has remained in being and still, after more than a half-century, is an active force in every major phase of civic affairs. The Cincinnatus Association forced a reorganization of the government from top to bottom, and helped to bring about the adoption by the citizens in 1924 of a Municipal Charter. The city still operates under this Charter, as amended several times by popular vote, and hence over many decades has served as a model of clean, efficient, and financially responsible city government. The governmental structure is of the city-manager type, with legislative authority in the hands of a small, elected City Council presided over by a mayor who has no special powers, and administrative authority lodged in an appointed city manager.

As the twentieth century moved into the 1920s and beyond, the growth rate of the city slowed, at least until major downtown renewal efforts were launched in the 1960s and reached a high point in the 1970s. During the slowing period, Cincinnati came to be surpassed by such cities as Cleveland, Chicago, Los Angeles, Detroit, Atlanta, and Houston in rate of population growth, in economic importance, and as a center of transportation. World War I was s strongly traumatic experience for a community, many thousands of whose residents were removed only a generation or two from Germany and were proud of their German heritage. Prohibition dealt a crippling below to Cincinnati's major brewing and distilling industries.

Because of its greatly diversified industry, and its general economic conservatism, Cincinnati suffered less than most American cities during the Great Depression after 1929. Since World War II, however, many of its major industries, hitherto locally owned, have been absorbed by large national

26

corporations and become subsidiaries, with the several disadvantages that usually are a by-product of absentee ownership.

Like most northern cities, Cincinnati had an influx during and after World War II of many Southern Blacks and Appalachian Whites. The newcomers, unlike the immigrants of an earlier day who moved into a less complex environment than that of the 1950s, have found it somewhat more difficult than their predecessors to become absorbed in the common life of the community. Again like other large cities, Cincinnati has experienced a flight to the suburbs, with all the problems that customarily follow in its wake: a shrinking tax base coupled with a steadily increasing demand for ever more costly municipal services, urban decay, a lessening sense of community, and the like.

Nonetheless, there remain an enviable continuity and stability in the life of this old city that too many American cities lack. Many of the lineal descendants of American and foreign immigrants of a century or a century-and-a-half ago, still provide leadership in politics, business, and cultural affairs. With less fuss and bitterness than elsewhere, Cincinnatians, black and white, supported a black vice mayor in 1955, and chose a black mayor in December 1972.

Moreover, an unusual number of local civic clubs, formed many years ago to foster Cincinnati's civic, economic, and cultural life, exert a strong influence even today. Aside from the Cincinnatus Association, these include the Commercial Club (1880), the Optimists of the Queen City Club (1890), and the Commonwealth Club (1917). The bicentennial celebration activities served to stimulate a new sense of unity and to give additional impetus to urban renewal downtown, to the revitalization and beautification of the riverfront, and to the offering of cultural and artistic opportunities and enjoyment to an ever broader segment of the populace.

In short, despite the vicissitudes shared with the rest of the United States and, indeed, with the whole world, Cincinnati has retained its special character as an eminently livable city; not too large; not too small; inclined to be conservative because of a widespread and strong sense of the past; ready to accept, not merely to tolerate, the new when it seems reasonable; enjoying cultural and recreational amenities not to be found in many larger metropolitan areas; with a power structure and business leadership characterized by a deep sense of civic obligations; governed by a reasonably efficient, clean, and responsive city government; and, above all, made up of a generally outgoing and friendly citizenry. Despite its problems and inequities, it is, as any solid Cincinnatian will tell you, a good place in which to work, to eat, to live, and to rear a family.

It may be amusing, in conclusion, to glance at two commentaries on Cincinnati made some 150 years apart.

In 1827, the Messrs. Benjamin Drake and Edward D. Mansfield published a booklet entitled *Cincinnati in 1826*. The authors call attention to the circumstance that, with each passing year, an increasing number of "those who are flying from southern heat and disease" in Mississippi, Alabama, and Louisiana have come to Cincinnati, with its "inviting aspect..., salubrious situation..., excellent schools..., cultivated society, many rational sources of amusement," and convenient transportation facilities. They "supposed" that, ere long, the wealthier visitors actually would have "their summer villas" here. The authors, among many other items, also listed some bargain prices for food and drink, to wit, 6 cents for a dozen eggs, 2 to 3 dollars for a hundredweight of beef, 12 cents for a bushel of corn, and 25 cents for a gallon of whisky! With charming candor, they did point to the lack of an umbrella factory in Cincinnati, but added that, "of the success of an establishment of this kind, there can be no doubt." In closing, they prophesied an inevitably prosperous future for their city.

And in December 1977, an article in *Advertising Age* magazine, while making no reference to Cincinnati's natural climate, made much of the city's climate of expansion and progress. "The expansion enthusiasm being generated," said the article, "is far from the conservative 'wait and see' philosophy which was the city byword for so many years. With the decision to build a modern stadium on the Ohio riverfront in 1967, Cincinnati made a move which unleashed a growth fervor which has intensified with the passage of time." As a consequence, the Queen City has come to "the forefront as a major metropolitan area— progressive, growth-oriented, culture-conscious, and aware of its assets and potential." Cincinnati, in short, a century and a half after the prophecy of the Messrs. Drake and Mansfield, had reached "one of the most potentially advantageous positions of any major city in the country."

THE PLATES

ALMS PARK AND "OH, SUSANNA"

When speaking of parks in Cincinnati and of their views, it is wise to be careful, for many of the residents have strong preferences. Nonetheless, it seems safe to say that one of the most charming is the Frederick H. Alms Memorial Park, given to the city during the period of World War I by Mr. Alms' widow.

It rests serenely atop a promontory, with municipally-owned Lunken Airport nearly 300 feet directly below. There are spectacular outlooks on the junction of the Little Miami and Ohio Rivers, and on the site at which Columbia, the first white settlement in Hamilton County, was established in 1788. At one time, the parkland area was called Bald Hill; Indians, it was said, had cut the original trees in order better to observe settlers coming down the river.

Fitting beautifully into the setting is the Stephen Collins Foster Memorial Statue, the work of Arthur Ivone. Presented to the city by Josiah Kirby Lilly, it was unveiled in 1937, in honor of a pioneer figure in Cincinnati's long musical tradition. Foster lived in Cincinnati from 1846 to 1850. He worked as a bookkeeper-clerk in his brother's wholesale commission house, spending many hours along the lively waterfront, with its wharves, riverboats, and roustabouts.

Although he was a competent clerk, Foster's real interest lay in tuneful music, and it was in Cincinnati that he established himself as a composer of popular songs. His best known melody dating from this period is "Oh, Susanna." Appropriately, the Alms Park statue has the composer of "My Old Kentucky Home" facing Kentucky.

THE ART ACADEMY AND THE "DUVENECK BOYS"

Cincinnati's eminence in the field of creative art is owing in no small measure to the Art Academy of Cincinnati. Its origins go back to the McMicken School of Art and Design, founded in 1869 by the trustees of the Charles McMicken Fund. This school, in effect, represented the first step in the development of McMicken University, which itself eventually became a component of the University of Cincinnati. Until 1873, the future academy occupied rented quarters; then, with more than 300 students, it moved into the nearby Cincinnati College Building at Fourth and Walnut Streets.

In 1884, the art school came under the control of the Cincinnati Museum Association, which was in the process of erecting an art museum in Eden Park. One year after the Cincinnati Art Museum opened in 1886, the art school, renamed the Art Academy of Cincinnati, held its first classes in an adjacent new building, as shown in the picture. The construction funds were provided largely by such civic-minded and art-conscious businessmen as Joseph Longworth, David Sinton, and Reuben R. Springer. Owing to extensive remodelings of both buildings, the Art Academy now is physically attached to the Art Museum.

Among the most famous teachers at the academy have been the sculptor, Louis Rebisso; the woodcarver, William Fry; the painters, Frank Duveneck and Herbert P. Barnett; and the pottery maker and woodcarver Benn Pitman—who originally came to Cincinnati from England in order to teach, and encourage the use of, a shorthand system developed by his brother, Sir Isaac Pitman.

Duveneck, of whom John Sargent said that he had the greatest brush talent in his generation, taught at the Art Academy over a period of three decades. When he opened a school in Munich, he soon had more than sixty students, a number of them Americans. These "Duveneck Boys" at first achieved notoriety as pranksters and gay blades, and then, in most cases, won distinction as painters.

Some of the most talented students of woodcarving were women. Their products decorated a number of houses in Cincinnati and elsewhere, and they provided the panels for the Music Hall's first organ. When this instrument was replaced, most of its carved panels were used to line the orchestra pit.

THE CINCINNATI ART MUSEUM: DARIUS TO DALI AND BEYOND

Outstanding among American art museums, particularly among those in medium-sized metropolitan areas, is the Cincinnati Art Museum. This cultural gem, in effect, is a legacy of the nation's centennial in 1876, and of the energy and imagination of a group of patriotic women art lovers. For, in the year following the opening of the Centennial Exposition in Philadelphia, members of the Cincinnati Women's Centennial Committee, some of whom had exhibited samples of their pottery and woodcarving at the fair, reorganized the group into the Women's Art Museum Association. The association members then persuaded friends to give or lend art objects, first for exhibition in some rented rooms, and then, it was hoped, in an art museum.

Their efforts bore rich fruit when, a few years later, Charles West gave $150,000 toward the construction of a museum, if an equal amount were acquired by popular subscription. The public responded generously. Thereupon, a Cincinnati Museum Association was created in 1881, the city contributed a museum site on the crest of a lovely hill in Eden Park, and the Cincinnati Art Museum was dedicated in 1886. Its first director was the native Cincinnatian, Sir Alfred T. Goshorn, who had organized the Philadelphia Exposition and who had been knighted by Queen Victoria for that achievement.

Originally, the building was a two-story Romanesque structure, a few parts of which still are visible. The classical portico in the photograph was added to the *back* of the structure in 1907, and was used as an employees' entrance to the Greek and Roman sections of the museum until after World War II! In 1946, the museum, in effect, was turned around, and the portico was designated as the main entrance.

The largesse of such donors as Mary M. Emery, Herbert Greer French, and Mary Hanna; the leadership and generosity of patrons such as John J. Emery; and the wise administration of directors such as Philip R. Adams have resulted in magnificent acquisitions of classical art, of masterpieces of western painting and sculpture, of Asiatic (particularly Near Eastern and Middle Eastern) treasures, and of fine prints and etchings.

36

THE CINCINNATI SKYLINE FROM KENTUCKY

Both economically and culturally, Greater Cincinnati extends beyond the Ohio borders into Southeastern Indiana and Northern Kentucky—the so-called Tri-State area. Some of the best views of the city, in fact, are available only from outside Ohio, particularly from Northern Kentucky. The view in the picture was taken from the Riverside Drive Historic District of Covington, Kentucky. Riverside Drive itself has many fine Victorian houses built by well-to-do individuals who sought the solitude of suburban hills combined with ready access to, and splendid views of, the city across the river, where many of them did and do work, shop, and attend cultural or recreational events.

CINCINNATI VIEWED FROM MOUNT ECHO PARK

None of Cincinnati's many parks overlooking the Ohio affords a better view of the river and of the city's basin than does Mount Echo Park, on the city's west side. Named for the reverberations emanating from its sheer, resonant cliff, Mount Echo is on the southeastern edge of Price Hill, which itself towers over the western edge of the basin in much the same way that Mount Adams does in the east. Its middle-class, heavily German-Catholic neighborhood, however, is somewhat more staid than that of Mount Adams.

Cincinnati prides itself on being a city of seven hills, though anyone familiar with the city easily can name seventeen eminences. Originally, as might be expected, the city was not built on hills. Instead, it began and grew in the basin area at the foot of the hills. By 1860, some 160,000 people were crowded into about two square miles, giving Cincinnati a greater population density at the time than had mid-nineteenth century Tokyo or New York. The move to the hills began in earnest after the Civil War. Then the basin area lost its residential character and gradually developed into the industrial and commercial hub of the city.

THE CINCINNATI ZOO, WHITE TIGERS, AND BEER KEGS

Founded largely through the interest and generosity of Andrew Erkenbrecher, the Cincinnati Zoo, the second oldest in the nation, was opened in 1875. In recent years it has established an international reputation for breeding rare and endangered species in captivity. Among many animals successfully bred at the Zoo are lowland gorillas (nine born by 1978), snow leopards, pigmy hippopotami, cheetahs, bongos, and Persian leopards.

Probably the most dramatic development in this area, however, has been the birth at the Zoo of seven of the approximately forty-four known (1977) white tigers in the world. White tigers are not albinos; they have developed from a recessive gene in some Bengal tigers. When fully grown, they weigh up to 500 pounds each, about 100 pounds more than the norm for orange Bengal tigers. The Zoo owns two specimens of this rare animal strain. Of the remaining five born in Cincinnati, three belong to the National Zoo in Washington and a pair to John Cuneo's Hawthorne Circus; with both of these organizations, the Zoo had arranged breeding loans.

The clever people at the zoo have discovered that their white tigers delight in playing with a large aluminum beer keg. The male Bhim ("Great Fighter") strictly limits the time in which he allows his sister Sumita ("Good Friend") to join the fun.

DAYTON STREET, SOMETIME MILLIONAIRES' ROW

A number of elegant, Italianate houses were built, between 1860 and 1890, on Dayton Street in the city's West End. Then situated at the terminus of a streetcar line, the West End was the city's most fashionable neighborhood. The houses on Dayton Street, popularly called the Millionaires' Row of Cincinnati, were owned mainly by well-to-do brewers and meatpackers.

With the passing of years, the wealthy residents left their aging residences for more attractive housing on the city's hilltops, and, as often has happened in American cities, the social status of the newer occupants declined. In the late 1960s, however, the street became the target of a variety of beautification and preservation activities in a city increasingly aware of its past. The City Council, indeed, adopted an ordinance forbidding wreckers to wreck along a specified stretch of the street.

The façades of many of the old houses have been restored. Washington hawthorn trees, which lined the street in the nineteenth century, once again have been planted. One of the houses, that of the beer brewer, John Hauck, has been made into a house museum, operated by a local preservation group called the Miami Purchase Association for Historic Preservation. The Dayton Street Historic District, now the home largely of prideful black citizens, has been placed on the National Register of Historic Places. It bids fair to become a classic example of the dictum that preservation preserves neighborhoods, not merely houses.

44

DELTA QUEEN AND COLISEUM

The history of the Ohio River includes the saga of dozens of famous steamboats whose very names, such as *Island Queen*, arouse a glow of nostalgia. Cincinnati was the home port of more than 500 steamers in the pre-Civil War years, and, for several years, local steamship yards produced boats at the rate of one a week. Ironically, probably the best known Ohio riverboat was built abroad and first appeared on the Ohio River in 1947, long after the golden era of paddle-wheelers had passed.

The *Delta Queen* was assembled at Stockton, California, in 1926. Her hull was pre-fabricated in Scotland; shipped to Halifax in Nova Scotia; and sent to the West Coast by rail. For a decade and a half, the *Delta Queen*, and a sister (!) ship, the *Delta King*, ran as excursion boats between San Francisco and Sacramento. Then, during World War II, the vessels were used to ferry soldiers to troopships anchored outside San Francisco Bay. Sold as war surplus in 1947, the *Delta Queen* was purchased by the Greene Lines of Cincinnati. Since then, the *Delta Queen* has operated as the last of the old palatial overnight steamers on the inland waterways.

For several years, the *Delta Queen* has been exempted, by act of Congress, from certain regulations relating to the safety of overnight passenger boats. The future of the half-century-old sternwheeler is unclear, but the Delta Queen Steamboat Company, successor to the Greene Lines, in 1977 floated the new *Mississippi Queen*. Several times as large as the *Delta Queen*, she conforms to modern safety codes. But the place in history of the *Delta Queen*, steam calliope and all, seems secure. It is she who has kept alive the steamboat tradition on the Ohio.

In the background can be seen the 17,000-seat Riverfront Coliseum. It is used regularly for ice hockey and basketball games, and for such occasional events as rock concerts, circuses, rodeos, and religious crusades. In the far background are the Highland Towers apartment house, near the site of the former Highland House and the terminus of the old Mount Adams Incline, and the abandoned Holy Cross Monastery on the Mount's highest point.

46

THE DOWNTOWN SKYWALK: MUCH COLOR, NO CARS

So new is the name, if not the concept, of urban skywalks that it does not appear in even recently-published dictionaries. Yet in skywalks seems to lie the solution to a number of municipal core area problems, particularly those related to traffic.

The Cincinnati skywalk system is planned so that it eventually will link most parts of the central business district with above-street walkways. Some of the sections already built are lined with entrances to stores and offices, and even a cinema, as an added inducement for their use by shoppers. (So, to some extent, were medieval European covered bridges!) In addition, the elevated walkways have comfortable benches, and during the spring and summer months one frequently sees "brown-baggers" enjoying luncheon on a skywalk, singly, in pairs, and in larger groups.

The skywalk portion shown in the photograph is the one behind a major department store near Fountain Square; it shows another innovation aimed at making the downtown area more attractive, namely, the colorful "urban-wall project." The idea stemmed locally from Carl Solway and Jack Bolton, young men much interested in contemporary art and urban beautification. Launched in 1971, and involving mainly private financing, the project has led to some interesting results. Altogether, by the beginning of 1978, some thirteen building exteriors and one roof had been painted with brightly colored and sometimes humorous designs. The wall shown here was designed by a member of the Graphic Design Department in the College of Design, Art, and Architecture of the University of Cincinnati.

48

FINDLAY MARKET AND AN INDIAN CHIEF

Findlay Market, in the so-called Over-the-Rhine area, remains today the last survivor of the half-dozen market houses that were built in Cincinnati during the nineteenth century. The idea of this market dates from the 1830s, when General James Findlay, owner of considerable land north of Cincinnati (that is, north of the present Liberty Street), recorded the plat of the "Northern Liberties" and designated a portion thereof as Findlay's Market Square.

There the matter rested until 1849. Then, because the Northern Liberties and other nearby areas had become a haven for those who wished to evade Cincinnati's "blue laws," and because many of the German immigrants in the late 1840s settled there, the city annexed the region. After the death of Findlay's last heir, the executors of his estate gave the Market Square section to the city. Grading, paving, and work on a market building began promptly.

The first Findlay Market (1852) was little more than an iron shed, with meats, produce, dairy products, and delectable specialties exposed to the elements and flies. Half a century later, and again in 1915, the stalls were enclosed, and refrigeration and sanitary equipment were installed. In 1974, with the inspiration provided by bicentennial celebration, the market was completely redone, to look as it does in the picture. At the same time, it was designated as the Findlay Market Historic District. The 125th anniversary in 1977 was marked by music, parades, and gay festivities.

Many of the market's indoor stalls are leased and tended by fourth- and fifth-generation descendants of the German, Irish, and Italian ancestors who were the first lessees. The sale of fruits and vegetables is conducted mainly in the so-called outdoor stalls. These spaces are used by growers who come to town on specific days with their wagons, vans, and trucks. A sizable number of these vendors are newer on the scene and include persons of diverse national origins. One of them, interestingly, is an Oklahoma Indian Chief regularly attired in bib overalls. He first appeared there in 1970, when another vendor to whom he had lent some money settled the debt by turning over his business to the Chief. Once sickened by eating an unripe pawpaw, and himself disliking fruit, he now sells fruit at the Findlay Market.

50

FOUNTAIN SQUARE AND THE "GENIUS OF WATER"

The Queen City's equivalent of European grand plazas is Fountain Square, in the heart of the downtown district. Since 1871 it has symbolized the city's civic heart. It is here that Cincinnatians gather to celebrate, to protest, or simply to sit in the sun, perhaps with a lunch sack, and watch the world go by while listening to entertainment provided by the Recreation Commission.

Dominating the square is the 24-ton bronze Tyler Davidson Memorial Fountain, cast in Munich. It stands 43 feet high and its figures portray the varied uses of water. On the top pedestal is the "Genius of Water," represented by a draped woman nine feet tall and with arms outstretched in a pose of invocation. The figure is a favorite resting place of pigeons and starlings. Henry Probasco, a leading businessman, gave the fountain to the city as a memorial to his brother-in-law and business partner.

The first site of the fountain was donated to the county, which later gave it to the city, as a market place for butchers—the Fifth Street Market. The butchers tried to prevent the tearing down of their stalls on the ground that a fountain would not satisfy the gift requirement that the land be used for market purposes or else revert to the descendants of the donors. When their suit was denied on a technicality, the butchers refused to move; thereupon the City Council had the market dismantled in a single night. To maintain the fiction that the site still served as a market, however, the city's mayor annually for many years purchased a flower at the flower stand visible in the lower right part of the picture.

By the 1960s, it was obvious that Cincinnati had outgrown the popular assembly place. Hence, as a phase of the city's urban-renewal project, the fountain was moved, the square was enlarged, and a municipal parking garage was built beneath it. The fountain, turned around and situated about 35 feet from its first location, was rededicated in 1971, a century after its original dedication. In the photograph can be seen also the lower portion of the Fifth-Third Bank Center's Dubois Tower, named after the chemical firm that has its headquarters in the building.

GARFIELD PLACE: TWO PRESIDENTS IN BRONZE

It was not until 123 years after the brothers John and Benjamin Piatt donated a piece of parkland to the city that the approximately one acre of green officially was named Piatt Park. The gift was made in 1817; the name was bestowed in 1940.

This oldest of Cincinnati's parks sits in the middle of a busy section of Eighth Street. Extending two long blocks from Vine to Elm Streets, the section is known as Garfield Place. The Vine Street entrance is marked by a bronze equestrian statue by Louis Rebisso of William Henry Harrison. In consequence of a number of "snafus," the statue languished in the basement of a National Guard Armory for several years before being dedicated in 1896. A one-time commandant of Fort Washington, Harrison lived in North Bend, a few miles west of Cincinnati. He was Clerk of Courts for Hamilton County when he was elected President in 1840. It was his misfortune to die of pneumonia within a month after taking office; the illness resulted from exposure during his inaugural address, which ran on for an hour and forty minutes.

Near the middle of the park stands a bronze statue by Charles Niehaus of President James A. Garfield. When unveiled in 1887, it stood on a high pedestal in the intersection of Garfield Place and Race Street. After hindering buggy and motor car traffic for 28 years, the statue in 1915 was moved out of the crossing to the park itself.

The Tudor Gothic structure on the left side of the photograph is the Doctors' Building (recently renamed the Garfield Building), a medical-office complex dating from the early 1920s. The modern Garfield Towers serve as a combination apartment- and office-building. The large building on the right side of the picture is the 10-story limestone Cincinnati Club. It was opened in 1924 a as symbol of the ambitions and aggressiveness of the younger businessmen in the community.

In the background is the Covenant-First Presbyterian Church, built in 1875. Among the congregations that went into the formation of the present church body is the First Presbyterian Church, organized in 1790. The spires in the distance are those of the Plum Street Temple, the Cathedral of St. Peter in Chains, and the City Hall.

54

GASLIGHTS IN THE SNOW

Story has it that residents in the suburb of Clifton agreed to annexation by Cincinnati only after the city promised that the area could keep its street gaslights. In reality, Clifton was annexed in 1896, probably against the wish of a majority of its inhabitants, by the *combined* vote of the populations of Cincinnati and Clifton. But the legend does underscore Clifton's concern for its distinctiveness, and the residents' continuing affection for their several hundred remaining gaslights—some of which, with beautifully decorated iron poles, date from the 1840s. (Although most are in Clifton, there are gas lamps in other parts of the city, for a grand total of about eleven hundred.)

The village of Clifton, named after a farmstead, was incorporated in 1850, when it had some 585 residents. Because it sat on a high hill, its residents who wished to go to the city had to cope with the steep route down Vine Street. Until about 1900, Clifton remained essentially an exclusive residential community dominated by the palatial estates of the so-called Clifton Barons—barons largely of beer and oil.

The population gradually began to change after the move of the University of Cincinnati to a campus on the edge of Clifton in 1895. Today many Cliftonites have direct ties to the University, as students, faculty members, administrators, and suppliers. Since then, too, Clifton has become the medical center of Cincinnati, with the University's College of Medicine and several hospitals within or near its boundaries.

But even the newer population has developed pride in the area's residental charm. And part of this charm lies in the continuing presence of street gaslights, when most of the city's other streets are lighted by electricity. At various times during the past score of years, City Hall has considered conversion from gas to electricity, on the ground that this would bring an annual saving of some $65,000; on the other hand, it probably also would reduce real-estate values and thus adversely affect sale prices and tax returns. In any case, the Cliftonites regularly have mobilized strong opposition, wearing "Keep the Gaslights" buttons, crowding hearings at City Hall, and making effective use of communications-media support. The future fate of the lamps, however, is unsure, for most recently federal and state energy regulations have become a looming threat to their existence.

56

GAZEBO IN THE "GARDEN OF EDEN"

It has no signs warning visitors to "keep off the grass," this Eden Park on Mount Adams. Its nearly 200 acres of rolling hills overlooking the Ohio River once comprised the vineyard "Garden of Eden," belonging to the real-estate magnate, Nicholas Longworth.

Probably the most popular of the city's parks, it offers free summertime musical concerts and is the site of the Cincinnati Art Museum, the Art Academy of Cincinnati, the Cincinnati Historical Society, the Playhouse-in-the-Park, the Cincinnati Museum of Natural History, and the Irwin M. Krohn (botanical) Conservatory. There also is a stunning 12-acre artificial lake, called Mirror Lake, resting on a concrete shield covering a reservoir.

The gazebo shown in the picture is a springhouse, constructed in 1905 over a spring once thought to have had medicinal value. It is estimated that at one time the equivalent of 100 barrels of water per day was taken from the spring by health-minded Cincinnatians, many of whom drove to the park in carriages and enjoyed a social hour with their friends as they sipped the questionable elixir. In 1912, the Board of Health declared the water contaminated, and the spring was covered. The Moorish gazebo, with its interestingly scalloped arches, remains as a beautifully-placed open-sided shelter.

The Cincinnati appreciation of historical tradition is manifested in a number of well-kept memorial groves. These honor, through labeled trees, the Presidents of the United States, several dozen pioneer settlers, and distinguished American authors. A Heroes Grove of large oaks is dedicated to the memory of the soldiers at Valley Forge. A graceful Capitoline Wolf Statue, presented to Cincinnati by the Italian Government in 1931, is a bronze copy of the original in Rome.

Truly, the colorful spring flowers, the summer breezes, the golden trees of fall, and the soft snow of winter make the park a year-'round attraction for natives and visitors alike.

58

GLENDALE DEPOT—AND POTTING SHED

The key to the development of the outer suburbs of Cincinnati understandably has been transportation access to the central city. In the nineteenth century, such access was provided by numerous small railroads. And so it happened that, in 1855, in a train station of the Cincinnati, Hamilton, and Dayton Railroad, the village of Glendale was founded by a group of well-to-do Cincinnatians who purchased 600 acres of land in a parklike setting. The Glendale depot, just off the village square, ever since has been looked upon as one of the more important buildings in this upper-class suburb. Actually, though it seems to bother no one, the original structure was destroyed by fire in 1880; the building seen in the photograph was erected on the same site shortly thereafter.

With the advent of automobiles and a corresponding decline in passenger rail traffic, the station eventually was abandoned by the Baltimore and Ohio Railroad system, which had purchased it from the original owners. Like a number of the depots in the Greater Cincinnati area, the Glendale station has continued a precarious existence as a recycled building. Until recently, it served, as indicated by the sign visible in the picture, as a flower shop, "quaintly" called the Potting Shed. Today, the building is vacant, except for the presence of a small railroad switching-station crew.

INDIAN HILL: QUAINT SCHOOLHOUSE TO QUAINTER MUSEUM

When the now quaint-looking "little red schoolhouse" opened in the present Cincinnati suburb of Indian Hill in 1873, it was known as the Washington School. A typical Ohio rural school, it provided the rudiments of education to the children of not-very-prosperous farming families for a number of decades. Shortly before World War II, the school was closed and the building, until 1973, served variously as administrative headquarters for the local school board, a dance pavilion, and a community center.

Meanwhile, much of the hilltop area with its beautiful scenic views had been acquired by well-to-do families from Cincinnati proper and by top business executives transferred to the city. In a number of instances, the new residents continued to maintain working farms on their extensive estates and, until relatively recently, casual talk on the Hill frequently concerned itself with both crops and stocks. Today the Village of Indian Hill is one of Cincinnati's wealthiest fashionable suburbs; its citizens play a leading role in the business, professional, and cultural life of the Queen City.

As the nation's bicentennial year approached, a group of citizens organized the Indian Hill Historical Museum Association. Its objective was to recall the heritage of the area by restoring the building, of red brick on a gray stone base, as nearly as possible to its original form; by furnishing it with period memorabilia; and by using it as a museum for annual historical displays.

In the process of restoration, ten coats of paint had to be removed before the original interior was revealed. When the later slate blackboards were taken off, there came to light black plaster sheets that had been treated with lamp black, beer, and horse hair. On some of these old boards were found children's names and class schedules. In July 1975, the attractive and quaint little schoolhouse was rededicated as the even quainter Indian Hill Museum. The first, and highly successful, exhibit was a showing of Henry F. Farny's great Indian paintings, most of them borrowed from private collections. Born in Alsace, Farny was brought to Cincinnati as a child by his parents.

THE KROHN CONSERVATORY AT EASTERTIME

One of Cincinnati's most popular attractions, to both tourists and residents, is the Irwin M. Krohn Conservatory in Eden Park, a beautifully-kept public greenhouse. The current structure, opened in 1933, is the third greenhouse on its site. The first, built in the 1890s, was a small propagating house for the city's parks, although the public was welcome to come in and see the flowers. The second, built in 1903, was larger, and designed to house both a propagating house and a plant museum. The third, named for a generous and long-time member of the Cincinnati Park Board, and enlarged and remodeled several times, was built specifically as a public greenhouse. Propagating for the flowers in the city's parks now is done in other greenhouses.

The Conservatory's seasonal displays, particularly those at Christmas and Easter, have become its most popular attractions. The cross and lily arrangements at Eastertime occasionally arouse some objections. Since the Krohn Conservatory is under the jurisdiction of the Cincinnati Park Board, there is some feeling that, as a government agency, it should not sponsor a display with a religious motif. But this does not disturb the vast majority of Cincinnatians who, with their families, visit the greenhouse each Easter Sunday by uncounted thousands. There also is a beautiful annual Christmas display of the Child in the stable manger, with live farm animals; donated by a leading local firm, it attracts and fills with wonder tens of thousands of children brought by their parents during December.

64

THE LITERARY CLUB: "HERE COMES ONE WITH A PAPER"

This charming house on East Fourth Street, vintage 1820, is the home of The Literary Club of Cincinnati, one of the city's more remarkable and most venerable institutions. It was founded late in 1849 by 25 young Cincinnatians, including Rutherford B. Hayes, as a debating society and an association before which literary compositions were to be read and conviviality was to be enjoyed. The debates were eliminated in 1864 because they had come to be in violation of the club's tradition of non-activism in any sphere. The group's motto, "Here Comes One with a Paper," was taken from Shakespeare's *Love's Labour's Lost*.

Except for a 17-month hiatus during the Civil War, during which, as has been indicated in the text, all 51 members of the club volunteered for military service, the group for more than a century met every Monday night in the year, unless Christmas and New Year's Eves fell on that day. Today meetings are held on Mondays from early September to early June, because there is no air-conditioning system in the clubhouse.

In 1875, the membership total was set at 100. Admission to the club is by invitation only, following careful screening of a proposed candidate in the areas of literary skill, congeniality, and ability to attend fairly regularly. Women (wives only) have been admitted to the hallowed precincts only twice in history, once for a special dinner on the club's 100th anniversary, and again, for an inspection tour on its 125th anniversary. The only woman ever permitted to attend a regular meeting was the widow of member Everard Jack Appleton when she gave the club for its library the stained-glass window saved when Harvard University razed its Appleton Chapel. Among the more prominent members have been Salmon P. Chase, Murat Halstead, Thomas Buchanan Read, Rutherford B. Hayes, Cleveland Abbe, Carl W. Blegen, Nelson Glueck, George B. McClellan, Bellamy Storer, William Howard Taft, and Charles Phelps Taft (who donated the present clubhouse in 1930).

At each meeting, one of the members reads an original paper of from 30 to 45 minutes' length. Longer readings tend to remind the listeners of the next line from the same Shakespearian play: "God give him the grace to groan." On the average, this amounts to one paper per member every 24 or 30 months. A pleasant collation and informal discussions around tables complete the program. In some ways, the Literary Club is the last bit of true Victorianism in the Midwest.

LYTLE PARK AND THE TAFT MUSEUM

The continuity between the old Cincinnati and the new is manifested, perhaps clearer than elsewhere, along Fourth Street. And at the eastern end are lovely Lytle Park (under which runs an expressway) and the Taft Museum, housed in a gracious Early Federal white-frame mansion built in 1820 for Martin Baum, one of Cincinnati's early German immigrants and capitalists.

Lytle Park, actually an attractively landscaped plot covering about an acre, rests on the site of another mansion, once owned by the Lytle Family. For three generations before the Civil War, the Lytles played an important role in the city's political and social life. But the last male member of the family, the lawyer, poet, and Brigadier General William Haines Lytle, lost his life in the Battle of Chickamauga. Eventually, in 1905, the land became city property and was converted into a public green. Among other features, the park has a fine statue of an unbearded Abraham Lincoln by George Grey Barnard. Mr. and Mrs. Charles P. Taft, who had moved into the former Baum house in 1873, brought the statue to Cincinnati and gave it to the city in 1917.

For many years the Tafts entertained the great of two continents in their elegant home. And it was on its portico steps that William Howard Taft, half-brother of Charles (a newspaper publisher), was informed officially of his nomination for the Presidency in 1908.

In 1927, at Mrs. Taft's suggestion, there was founded the Cincinnati Institute of Fine Arts to stimulate musical and artistic education in the community. The generous couple then offered their house, its splendid art collections, and a million dollars, if a comparable contribution were made by the public. The citizens met the challenge, the Institute began its formal planning, and with the help of a second million-dollar Taft gift, the house was restored according to a color print of 1857. The Taft Museum then was opened to the public in 1932. It contains many masterpieces of painting, antique furniture and fine collections of French enamel, majolica ware, porcelain, and crystal.

Visible in the photograph behind the Museum is Mount Adams, pictured elsewhere, and the Church of the Immaculate Conception. This was consecrated six years to the day following the reaffirmation of the dogma of Immaculate Conception by Pope Pius IX in 1854.

MOUNT ADAMS: ALPINE VILLAGE AND GREENWICH VILLAGE

The history of this hill, long known as Mount Ida, goes back to the 1790s. It was said that Ida Martin, a washerwoman for Fort Washington, first lived there in a hollow sycamore. The first road, now known as Hill Street, probably was laid in 1793 by the Reverend Mr. James Kemper as a short cut between his Presbyterian church in town and the easterly farm bought for him by the congregation.

About 1830, the hill was acquired by Nicholas Longworth, who converted it into the vineyard, "Garden of Eden." In 1843, he donated four acres of the land to the Cincinnati College, so that an observatory could be built for Professor Ormsby M. Mitchel (*sic*). The public supplied some funds and many hours of labor, and former President John Quincy Adams, who once had been laughed at for proposing a series of national observatories, which he called "lighthouses of the sky," was invited to speak at the cornerstone laying in the same year. He accepted, and made the trip from Boston to Cincinnati in 13 days. Soon thereafter, Mount Ida was renamed Mount Adams. Eventually, this first "true" astronomical observatory in the United States was moved near Mount Lookout, where the air was cleaner.

With its many narrow boxlike houses and steep streets, Mount Adams still resembles an Alpine village. Because of its closeness to the Art Academy and Art Museum, and its marvelous views, it long has attracted teachers and students of art. As the older residents left or died, the houses were allowed to deteriorate and the area became markedly bohemian. During the 1960s, its Greenwich Village atmosphere made it popular with the so-called hippies. Most recently, however, there have been energetic "renewal" activities, as buyers and developers have become aware of the splendid views, the informal atmosphere, and the wonders that outside painting and inside remodeling could achieve with the well-built old houses.

The Church of the Immaculate Conception (1860) can be reached from the basin area by a very long set of concrete steps. Traditionally Catholics climb the steps between midnight of Maundy Thursday and noon on Good Friday.

MUSIC HALL: "GRAND OLD LADY"

As Cincinnati's "Grand Old Lady" among auditoriums, the century-old Music Hall, is one of the most beloved buildings in the community. Its architectural style is High Victorian Gothic, though soon after the red-brick building's completion, some snide fellow described its form as being "Sauerbraten Byzantine."

Music Hall sits on the site of the old German *Sängerhalle*, where the first two Cincinnati Choral Music Festivals were held, in May 1873 and May 1875, respectively. A number of patrons adjudged the wooden hall, with its tin roof that was noisy when it rained, to be inadequate for so grand a performing group. Among these patrons was Reuben R. Springer, a retired merchant. Himself offering $125,000, he also promptly organized, with John Shillito and others, a successful fund-raising campaign for the erection of a new hall with proper acoustical qualities; among the contributions were thousands of pennies, nickels, and dimes from school children.

The central portion of the Music Hall (Springer Hall), which now has some 3600 seats and excellent acoustics, was opened in time for the (third) May Festival in 1878. The later wings, North Hall and South Hall, with a commendable and profitable eclecticism variously have served as convention centers, exhibition halls, boxing and wrestling auditoriums, ice-skating rinks, ballrooms, and settings for tennis matches, auto shows, and "homeramas."

The "Grand Old Lady" has been metamorphosed internally several times during her long life. Most recently, Ralph and Patricia Corbett had the central hall elegantly redone, without impairing the excellent acoustics. They also provided, in the tower, a pleasant pre- and post-performance entertainment facility. The structure today houses the Cincinnati Symphony Orchestra, the Cincinnati Summer Opera, the May Festival, and the Cincinnati Ballet Company.

Over a century and more, most of the world's greatest musical artists, at one time or another, have appeared in the Music Hall. Wisely, the committee in charge of the centennial concert in May 1978, decided not to repeat the opening concert of 100 years ago; that one lasted for four hours and a half.

PADDLEWHEEL AND CITY LIGHTS

Where else but in Cincinnati would a towboat captain make a present of the vessel to his wife so that she could convert it into a successful restaurant? This is precisely what happened some years ago with the *Mike Fink*, moored on the Kentucky side of the river across from downtown Cincinnati. As a "river theme" restaurant, it has become popular with Kentuckians and Cincinnatians alike.

And who else but my colleague, Julianne Warren, would think of photographing Cincinnati at night by shooting between the buckets of the *Mike Fink's* paddlewheel?

At any rate, seen from the Kentucky shore as lighted buildings in the picture, by courtesy of the paddlewheel, are, from left to right: The Central Trust Tower, formerly the Union Central Life Insurance Company building; the 547-feet high Carew Tower, a 48-story office building; and the building of the Cincinnati Gas & Electric Company, standing on the spot where Cincinnati's first white child, William Moody, was born in 1790.

74

PLUM STREET TEMPLE, "CHARMING ODDITY"

Directly across the street from the Archdiocesan Cathedral of St. Peter in Chains stands the most famous of the city's synagogues, the Isaac M. Wise Temple, popularly known as the Plum Street Temple. Built of orange-colored stone in 1865-1866 for the B'nai Yeshurun Reform Jewish Congregation, the temple is a fine example of Moorish Gothic architecture. The "charming oddity" of this architectural style achieved some popularity in nineteenth-century design, for, as the French and German Gothic legacy of the Middle Ages appealed to nineteenth-century Christians, so did the Moorish Gothic form carry a reminder of the important role of the Jewish community in Moslem-ruled medieval Spain.

Dr. Isaac M. Wise, the Rabbi of the congregation from 1853 to 1900, is generally recognized as the father of Reform Judaism in the United States. Calling himself "an American born in Bohemia," he was convinced that Judaism in the Americas should be American in scope and have a ritual suited to the American environment. To this end, he founded the Hebrew Union College in Cincinnati in 1875, and served as president of this oldest Jewish theological school in the Americas until his death in 1900. The first rabbis ordained in the United States were ordained at the Plum Street Temple.

76

THE RIVERFRONT STADIUM AND "HAMMERING HANK"

A massive symbol of the city's riverfront renaissance in the late 1960s and 1970s is the Riverfront Stadium, built on the site of the city's founding. Plans for a stadium on the riverfront were included in the city's 1948 Master Plan, for the Cincinnati Reds frequently had expressed interest in having a playing facility larger than Redland Field—which was built in the West End in 1912 with 30,000 seats, and which was renamed Crosley Field when control of the club went to Powel (*sic*) Crosley, Jr., in 1934. Actual work on a new stadium was postponed, however, until the city began bidding for a professional football team in the 1960s.

It soon became clear that a new and very large stadium was a *sine qua non* for professional football. Hence, despite some controversies over location and financing, the city began pressing ahead with plans for, and work on, a suitable riverfront facility. The well-designed and expensive structure was ready for use in July 1970. The photograph shows an early game in the stadium between the Reds and the Atlanta Braves, whose great slugger, Henry Aaron, quickly became a part of Riverfront Stadium lore. "Hammering Hank" hit the first home run in the new stadium during the first game played there, the 1970 All-Star contest. Riverfront Stadium also was the site of Aaron's 714th home run, which tied the immortal Herman (Babe) Ruth's career mark, on Opening Day in 1974.

The stadium has been an auspicious place for Cincinnati sports. By the close of 1977, the Reds had won four National League pennants and two World Series since they began playing in the facility—and this despite the fact that the ball park is less than ideally suited to the team's style of play. It was 1973 before the Reds won more games at Riverfront Stadium than they did on the road. The other regular tenant, the Cincinnati Bengals of the National Football League, by the end of 1977 had reached the American Football Conference playoffs three times since they began playing at the stadium in 1970.

78

THE SERPENTINE WALL AND YEATMAN'S COVE

Well in line with local tradition in such matters, the Cincinnati Bicentennial Observance got off to a slow start before developing into a vigorous celebration with broad popular participation. Among its lasting achievements, once more underscoring the place of the river in the life of Cincinnati, was the erection (1976) of a massive concrete Serpentine Wall along the waterfront.

Built up from a natural amphitheatre at the head of an inlet, the wall, with a tiered seating capacity of several thousands, is part of a new development called Yeatman's Cove Park, although the nearby Riverfront Stadium covers the actual cove of that name. The Serpentine Wall rapidly has become the focal area for fireworks displays, singing groups, magic shows, operatic performances—and picnics by families interested in viewing the river and its boating and shipping activities. The park itself is adjacent to the Public Landing, where the *Delta Queen* docks on its trips to Cincinnati. The picture also shows the Showboat *Majestic* and the Suspension Bridge.

Yeatman's Cove itself was the name attached to the landing spot for the settlers who, coming downriver by boat in 1788, founded Losantiville, the later Cincinnati. It was named after Virginia-born Griffin Yeatman who, in 1793, began to operate what soon became a celebrated tavern, the "Square and Compass," just upriver from the cove. In the upper room of the tavern were held the first session of the Northwest Territory legislature and of the Ohio Supreme Court, as well as the first meeting of the Cincinnati Town Council. The busy, "wet," and noisy, "Square and Compass" in due time also housed the town's first post office, first museum, and first hospital ward.

80

THE SHOWBOAT *MAJESTIC*

For many Americans who lived in small towns along the great rivers in the 19th and early 20th centuries, the only contact with theatre was the annual visit of the showboat; somehow, there still is something irresistibly appealing about the immediacy of a play production in the cramped confines of a floating theatre, with ushers and barmaids in period costume.

The Showboat *Majestic*, permanently anchored at Cincinnati's Public Landing, was built in 1923, under commission from Captain Tom Reynolds, one of the last of the old-time showboaters. Like most later showboats, the *Majestic* is a barge; before coming to rest in Cincinnati, she was pushed from one to another of her many stops on the Ohio and Kentucky river systems by a towboat. Showboating obviously declined in the 20th century, as automobiles made theatre in the cities more accessible to the residents of small-town America and as motion pictures effectively competed with all live theatre. The *Majestic* herself, indeed, was mothballed for a time; but in the early 1950s, Hiram College in Ohio, and later Indiana University, took over the boat and used her as a floating training school for theatrical students. In 1967, the vessel was acquired by the city of Cincinnati for public purposes, and the University of Cincinnati Theatre Department has successfully staged several plays on it each summer since 1968.

"STREET OF SPIRES": CATHEDRAL AND CITY HALL

Eighth Street is Cincinnati's "Street of Spires." On the west side of the intersection at Eighth and Plum Streets, rise two of the city's most imposing steeples atop two of its most important buildings.

The white spire in the picture foreground is that of the Roman Catholic Archdiocesan Cathedral of St. Peter in Chains, constructed in 1846 under the direction of Archbishop John B. Purcell. The gleaming white building, with its 221-feet-high steeple, generally is considered to be the outstanding Greek Revival building in the Cincinnati area. It is a depository for a number of important works of art, including Bartolomé Murillo's painting *St. Peter in Chains* (from which the building takes its name) and a crucifix with the corpus by Benvenuto Cellini. St. Peter in Chains lost its cathedral status in 1938, by which time the surrounding neighborhood had deteriorated. In 1951, however, Archbishop Karl J. Alter announced plans to remodel the structure and to restore its cathedral designation. The renovation, precursor of the city's downtown renaissance, was completed in 1957. The interior of the cathedral now is in harmony with the Greek motif of the exterior.

Across the street from the cathedral sits the Romanesque City Hall, of red granite. The building was completed in 1893, in the political heyday of "Boss" George B. Cox; it remains one of his most enduring legacies to the city. The graceful tower rises to a height of 253 feet, some 30 feet higher than the cathedral steeple. Designed by Samuel Hannaford, the interior of the City Hall is graced by carved marble staircases and allegorical stained glass windows. Most of the original murals in the building unfortunately have been painted over. Periodically, city officials complain about the building's antiquated facilities; but thus far the estimated expense of modernization has proved to be an inhibiting economic and political obstacle.

84

THE SUSPENSION BRIDGE, FORERUNNER OF THE BROOKLYN BRIDGE

When the Cincinnati-Covington (Kentucky) Suspension Bridge was opened for use on January 1, 1867, it was reputed to be the longest suspension bridge in the world. It was not the first bridge to span the Ohio River, but it is by far the longest-lived such structure.

A bridge project was talked about as early as 1815, but it was not until the 1840s that plans to bridge the Ohio were discussed in earnest. The steamboat captains generally were opposed to any bridge, fearing that it of necessity would be so low as to clip off their vessels' smokestacks; their negativism long delayed action on any specific proposal. Eventually, however, the Commonwealth of Kentucky, which, under the Northwest Ordinance of 1787 controls the river along the Ohio-Kentucky border, approved construction of a span. In 1857 the stone pillars for a bridge were put in place.

The Suspension Bridge Company soon ran into financial difficulty, and work on the project was suspended in 1859. It was resumed shortly after the Civil War, which had demonstrated clearly to Cincinnatians and Kentuckians alike the advantages of rapid access from the Queen City to the Kentucky Hills and vice versa, and was completed by 1867. Tolls were collected until the 1960s to recover construction costs.

The designer of the bridge was John A. Roebling, an engineering genius who advocated suspension of the bridge from steel cables, and who solved the problem of the bridge swaying in the wind by using cross stays on the steel ropes—two innovations that later came to be accepted as routine in bridge construction. Roebling's most enduring claim to fame was his design of the much longer Brooklyn Bridge, on which he started work soon after finishing the Cincinnati-Covington Bridge. Tragically, he died as the result of an accident before that bridge was finished in 1883. Eastern visitors to Cincinnati often comment that the Suspension Bridge looks like the Brooklyn span; historically, the fact is the other way around.

To the right of the Suspension Bridge in the photograph can be seen the Cincinnati Riverfront Stadium.

86

TOWBOAT: "WORKHORSE OF THE OHIO RIVER"

The romantic age of the river steamers is gone. Today, the queens of the Ohio River are the towboats and barges that annually transport tens of millions of tons of freight up and down the river—now a major channel of energy transportation. In 1970, about 59,000,000 tons of coke and coal, and 25,000,000 tons of crude oil and gasoline were shipped via the Ohio River.

Unlike the situation in the nineteenth century, when the river on occasion virtually dried up during the summer—in 1886, it measured under two feet at its deepest point in Cincinnati—and often was blocked by ice in the winter, the river today nearly always is navigable. During the 1920s, an extensive series of river locks and dams was built to ensure a pool nine feet deep at all times; recent modifications ensure a pool at least twelve feet deep; indeed, the river depth today rarely drops below twenty feet at Cincinnati. The greater depth normally helps to prevent a freezing-over during the winter, although it was possible to walk across the river on ice during the extremely cold weather in January 1977.

Modern dams along the feeder streams of the Ohio also have helped to limit the damage caused by flooding. It is not uncommon for the waters to rise above the present 52-feet flood level at Cincinnati, but more than two decades have passed since Third Street found itself under water.

THE UNIVERSITY OF CINCINNATI: "THE MOST BEAUTIFUL URBAN CAMPUS"

Some years ago, a leading encyclopedia spoke of the University of Cincinnati's site as being "the most beautiful urban campus" in the country. The praise doubtless was bestowed in part because of the years-long successful efforts to keep trees, grass, and flowers much in evidence despite the mushrooming growth of the physical plant. And occupying one of the most attractive spots on the main or Clifton Campus is McMicken Hall (shown in the picture), home of the College of Arts and Sciences.

As mentioned in the text, the University traces its origins to the privately-established Cincinnati College and the Medical College of Ohio, both dating from 1819. It was enlarged through mergers with a number of later schools, including McMicken University, and in 1870 became a municipally-supported institution. After further expansion in plant, students, and expenses, it became a state university in 1977. At the end of 1977, it had an enrollment of some 40,000 students and a plant value of close to $350,000,000.

The University of Cincinnati during its 159 years of existence has contributed some important "firsts" to society. The co-operative system of technical education, whereby students alternate terms in class and on practical jobs, was introduced to the world here in 1906. The safest and most effective polio vaccine, the Sabin vaccine, was developed in the University's Medical School. The first American textbooks in military surgery and in the treatment of radiation accidents were written here.

The use of a public hospital as a medical-college teaching hospital, the development of a baccalaureate program in nursing and health, and the development of the first effective antihistamine for human use (Benadryl), all are Cincinnati "firsts." So were the first completely ball-bearing-equipped building elevator and the first method of making safe a marketable anti-knock gasoline. Faculty members here devised the first program of computer training for the blind, and the most feasible means of providing adequate warmth at low cost for the armed services stationed along the Arctic DEW line. Finally, in this list but not in fact, the first method enabling the United States Navy to pin-point the position of submarines in the ocean, and the first and still widely-used commercial method for extracting ginger to make ginger ale came from the Clifton Campus.

90

WILLIAM HOWARD TAFT'S BIRTHPLACE

In this house in Cincinnati's Mount Auburn section, William Howard Taft was born on September 15, 1857. Cincinnati's only native son to become President of the United States, he is the only man ever to have served as both President of his country and Chief Justice of the Supreme Court. "Big Lug," as he was known as a youngster, also was the heaviest President, weighing some 350 pounds.

Over the years, his boyhood home, a two-story brick building built in 1853, became a four-family apartment building; eventually it was acquired by the United States Department of the Interior, which is converting it into a museum in Taft's honor. The National Park Service personnel who are charged with restoring the house to its original state face a difficult task, inasmuch as the building was remodeled following a fire in 1875.

XAVIER UNIVERSITY

Xavier University traces its origins to the founding of the Athenaeum by the first bishop of the Cincinnati Diocese, the strongly education-minded Bishop Edward Fenwick in 1831. Eventually the operation of the college was entrusted to the Society of Jesus. Situated on Sycamore Street, in the downtown area, from 1831 to 1918, the institution then was moved to its present site on an old golf course in Evanston, a suburb annexed to Cincinnati in 1911. The university (it was so named in 1930) has a distinguished record of academic service. In 1977, it had an enrollment of some 6,000 full- and part-time students, both men and women.

Visible in the picture are the steps leading from Victory Parkway to a small but charming statue of the Spanish missionary, St. Francis Xavier. In the background can be seen Hinkle Hall, erected in 1920 and used for many years as the Jesuit residence on the campus. When the Jesuit living quarters were moved in 1970 to the attractive new Walter E. Schott, Sr., Memorial Building, Hinkle Hall was converted to serve mainly as a faculty office building. Like many of the early structures on the campus, Hinkle Hall was designed in Tudor style, by Joseph G. Steinkamp and Brother.

Xavier University's motto is: "He has seen great wonders."